# DATE DUE

| | | | |
|---|---|---|---|
| | | | |
| | | | |
| | | | |
| | | | |
| | | | |
| | | | |
| | | | |
| | | | |
| | | | |
| | | | |
| | | | |
| | | | |

Bilingual Edition

# READING POWER

Edición Bilingüe

# Sammy Sosa

## Home Run Hitter
## Bateador de home runs

**Rob Kirkpatrick**

**Traducción al español**
Mauricio Velázquez de León

The Rosen Publishing Group's
PowerKids Press™ & **Buenas Letras**™
New York

For my Father.
Para mi Padre.

Published in 2002 by The Rosen Publishing Group, Inc.
29 East 21st Street, New York, NY 10010

**First Bilingual Edition 2002**
First Edition in English 2001

Book Design: Michael de Guzman

Photo Credits: p. 5 © Jonathan Daniel/Allsport; p. 7 © Michael Zito/SportsChrome USA; p. 9 © Steve Woltman/SportsChrome; p. 11 © Reuters/Adrees A. Latif/Archive Photos; p. 13 © Janice E. Rettaliata/Allsport; pp. 15, 22 Vincent Laforet/Allsport; p. 17,19 © Rob Tringali Jr./SportsChrome; p. 21 © Sporting News/Archive Photos.

Text Consultant: Linda J. Kirkpatrick, Reading Specialist/Reading Recovery Teacher

Kirkpatrick, Rob.
 Sammy Sosa: home-run hitter = Sammy Sosa : bateador de home runs / by Rob Kirkpatrick : traducción al español Mauricio Velázquez de León.
 p. cm.— (Reading Power)
 Includes bibliographical references and index.
 ISBN 0-8239-6132-X (alk. paper)
 1. Sosa, Sammy, 1968— Juvenile literature. 2. Baseball players— Biography— Juvenile literature. [1. Spanish language materials—Bilingual.] I. Title. II. Series.

GV865.S59 K57 1999
796.357'092–dc21
[B]

**Word Count:**
English: 123
Spanish: 139

Manufactured in the United States of America

# Contents ——

# —— Contenido

Sammy Sosa plays baseball. He is on the Chicago Cubs.

———

Sammy Sosa juega béisbol. Él juega en los Cachorros de Chicago.

Sammy plays in the outfield. He uses his glove to get fly balls.

———

Sammy usa un guante para atrapar batazos elevados en el jardín.

7

Sammy is number 21 on the Cubs.

———————

Sammy es el número 21 en los Cachorros.

9

Sammy is happy when his team wins. He gives "high fives" when his team wins.

———

Sammy se pone feliz cuando gana su equipo. Choca las manos con los otros jugadores para celebrar que su equipo ha ganado.

11

Sammy played for the Chicago White Sox. He liked to bat for the White Sox.

———

Sammy jugaba con los Medias Blancas de Chicago. A Sammy le gustaba mucho batear para aquel equipo.

13

Mark McGwire is friends with Sammy. Mark plays for the St. Louis Cardinals.

———————

Mark McGwire es amigo de Sammy. Mark juega en los Cardenales de San Luis.

Sammy hits a lot of home runs. Sammy hit 66 home runs in 1998.

----

Sammy batea muchos jonrones *(home runs)*. En 1998 Sammy bateó 66 jonrones.

Sammy likes to hit the ball.
He can hit it way up in
the air.

———

A Sammy le gusta batear.
Él puede batear la
bola muy lejos.

19

People like Sammy's smile.
He makes people happy.

———————

A la gente le gusta la
sonrisa de Sammy.
Él hace felices a muchas
personas.

**21**

The Sosa family loves Sammy. He likes it when they see his games.

---

La familia de Sammy lo quiere mucho. Sammy disfruta cuando van a verlo a sus partidos.

Here are more books to read about
Sammy Sosa:

Para leer más acerca de Sammy
Sosa, te recomendamos estos
libros:

*Sammy Sosa,* by Richard Brenner
William Morrow & Company (1999)

*Sammy Sosa,* by Laura Driscoll,
illustrated by Ken Call
Grosset & Dunlap (1999)

To learn more about baseball, check
out this Web site:

Para aprender más sobre béisbol,
visita esta página de Internet:

http://CNNSI.com/

# Glossary

**bat** (BAT) When a player stands by home plate and tries to hit the ball.

**fly ball** (FLY BAWL) A ball that a batter has hit way up in the air.

**home run** (HOHM RUHN) When a batter hits the ball out of the park and gets to run around the bases.

**outfield** (OWT-feeld) Part of a baseball field where right fielder, center fielder, and left fielder play.

# Index

# Glosario

**batazo elevado** Una bola que se ha bateado muy arriba en el aire.

**chocar las manos** Algo que hacen los jugadores para celebrar con un amigo o compañero de equipo .

**manopla (la)** Guante que usan los beisbolistas para atrapar la pelota.

**jardín (el)** Campo abierto. El lugar del campo de béisbol donde juegan los jardineros (derecho, central e izquierdo).

**jonrones / home runs** Cuando un jugador batea la pelota fuera del campo y corre alrededor de las cuatro bases.

# Índice